One of Seven Billion

One of Seven Billion

poems by

Tim Sherry

MoonPath Press

Poetry
ISBN 978-1-936657-14-8

Cover photo: "Reading Only Good News" by Peter Serko

Author photo: Peter Serko

Book design by Tonya Namura
using Minion Pro

MoonPath Press is dedicated to publishing the
best poets of the U.S. Northwest Pacific states

MoonPath Press
PO Box 1808
Kingston, WA 98346

MoonPathPress@yahoo.com

http://MoonPathPress.com

To Marcia, who knows what I need to hear
when it's really not about me.

Acknowledgments

Grateful acknowledgment is made to the editors of the following publications where these poems first appeared, some in slightly different forms:

Crab Creek Review, "Girl Walking in Wallace, Idaho"
Drash: Northwest Mosaic, "Stardust"
Floating Bridge Review #6 in the Pontoon section,
    "The Best Doughnuts in the World"
Interdisciplinary Humanities, "The Light"
Seminary Ridge Review, "Sometimes All You Can Do Is
    Just Wonder"
The Broad River Review, "Of Fires"
The Raven Chronicles, "The Bird Behind Jesus"
Windfall: A Journal of Poetry of Place, "Berry Picking in
    Puyallup, 1956"

The poem "wiffle ball was" appeared as a broadside created by Jessica Spring of Tacoma, Washington's Springtide Press as part of the November, 2008 Art At Work Project sponsored by the Tacoma Arts Commission.

The poem "Word Game with a Little Boy" appeared on the website *The Far Field: Washington State Poet Laureate Program * Washington State Poets and Poetry* in December of 2013.

Thanks to Charles and Jill at the Kangaroo House B&B on Orcas Island in Washington state's San Juan Islands where some of these poems were written during an Artsmith Artist Residency in March of 2010.

Deep gratitude to Derek Sheffield who first said my poetry had merit and to Allen Braden who has taught me so much

and to Kevin Miller who always has a kind word and to
Peter Ludwin who listens so well and to Michael Magee
who gives the best compliments and especially, especially
to Connie Walle who has been such a supportive mentor
and who has made The Puget Sound Poetry Connection
such a vital part of the Tacoma writing community.

Special thanks to Lana Hechtman Ayers without whose
support and encouragement in the last several years this
collection could not have happened.

Table of Contents

I am alone, I thought, and they are everybody.
—Fyodor Dostoyevsky,
Notes from the Underground

One of Seven Billion

wiffle ball was

fifteen paces
stepped off from the stoop
and a line scuffed
across the sidewalk

and a white plastic ball
with magic holes
and a yellow bat lighter
than Merlin's wand

and trees pointed to mark
the infield, the outfield,
a home run
and words thrown

to brag the moment
on afternoons
when we thought
we would live forever

I

Midland

There was no candlestick maker
at the crossroads where we lived. But there
was a butcher and a baker, and we called
all the businesses by someone's name.
Alex fixed our cars and told the best stories.
Roy had the Shell station for our gas
and green stamps. Baskett Lumber
was our hardware store. We got our groceries
at Bittner's, and Frank fixed our shoes.
Morrie delivered the mail, but the post office
was Marion behind the counter.
We were our parents' kids—
unless someone wanted to know our names
after a window was broken.

One road went west to the Mountain Highway
and east to the Catholic church. Our Main Street
was the road north to the Tacoma city limits
and south to the new high school.
A blinking red light was enough
excuse most days for dads to swing off to pick up
some cigarettes or get a beer at Little Vic's.
The Sears catalogue was as close to the big city
as moms got more than once or twice a year.
Saturday mornings everyone had something
they needed to call it downtown. It was a dot
in the middle of white space on the map; but
it was our place in the world where we learned
to handle any crossroads we would ever come to.

1954 Indian War

We all wanted to be Indians, secret,
roaming the woods half naked with our shirts off,
just so we could be half naked.
Cowboys on TV were too doozied up for us.
We gathered moss to tinder our fires
and romanced the hours into wigwams
of tree branches and stretched sheets.
The meat we dried was squirrels
too curious for their own good.
Our peace pipes were filled with cigarette butts
busted open. We wore finger paint
stolen from Sunday school
and stuck chicken feathers in the bandanas
holding Halloween hair that covered our crew cuts.
Carrots were dried roots as authentic as imagination.

When the parents heard about the tribe,
they acted like the cavalry
and shot our explanations full of holes.
They didn't just hate Indians.
They scolded us with stories from their parents
who had lived down the road from the reservation
and saw all the dead cars and sofas in the front yards,
all the bottles laying around.
They could barely sputter how stupid
the idea of sign language was.
They scoffed at us pretending such nonsense.
Why would we want to be like those savages?
Why not Marines? The Army?
They even had some old uniforms we could use—
and a genuine German Luger.

Berry Picking in Puyallup, 1956

The berry fields were the berry fields
and we were the pickers each day,
early, out even before loggers were in the woods,
waiting the busses rescued from school runs
with the lettering below the windows
painted out and a farmer's name stenciled.
The sun was so pure those mornings
we thought all Time was spreading for us
in its rise over Rainier
as we got our flats and lined the boxes
together with a final push of the corners,
our fingers still stained from the day before.

We started each row with a jacket
or a shirt laid down to mark our return
with another punch in the first card
we would carry with our name
on it. Lunch was peanut butter and jam
and white bread. Dessert was all day long
on berries hidden in a hand pretending a cough
or popped from a box when the field boss
looked away at someone's catcall.

Those three weeks of strawberries each summer
were the first freedom we had
to try out forbidden words,
to work for something more than allowance,
to think thoughts migrant beyond childhood
before we all pushed onto the bus for the ride
home into the sunset behind the smoke
spreading out above the lumber mills
across the tide flats of Commencement Bay.

Of Fires

August was the best month for melanoma—
when heat made tinder of the grass,
lightning glowed far off in the darkness,
and fires started in unseen places.
It was the year that Yellowstone burned;
and while the news was full of orange nights,
while all the world waited what to do,
a mole began to burn on his back.
The fires and debates raged in Wyoming;
and after we heard the doctor's careful words,
there was no fire policy to be asked.
Tom Carr looked away, and said to let it burn.
It was no fire engine fire with barking dogs
and people turning away to talk about the weather.
We were held by fear and fascination
as his disease burned before us.
The casseroles and cousins came in the back door.
Throughout the house his memories were gathered.
We ushered through the living room where his bed
was brought for the final wonder of it all;
and as we watched, it was over in four dread weeks.
No pictures of fires on the news compared.
It was day to day, hour by hour, and then
minutes each different as he was consumed.
On the last day, when all was gone but his breathing,
the news was still of Yellowstone on fire,
and the debate there had much to say about
the choice to let two hundred years of trees burn.
But after those weeks in August, what we watched
in Tom Carr filled us with such loathing and love
we knew of nothing to say of fires.

One of Seven Billion

I'm not good with numbers,
so the announcement
that the world population has reached
seven billion makes me nervous.
As the enumerator in a fraction
with that denominator,
I wonder if the right-to-lifers
really think any one soul
is as valuable as the next.
When I garden, it's the same.
I wonder if that carrot
is going to taste better than that one.
What makes one tulip
a better yellow than another?
I know obituaries
have to use hyperbole.
But compared to Lincoln
or Mother Theresa,
what will there be worth saying
about one more son, husband, father?
Any number ending with *I-O-N*
spins my head, and I wonder if
some distant god is laughing at me.
When someone emphasizes,
That's with a B,
I want to drive to a friend's house
and hope he invites me in
for a cup of coffee.

Wonderful Watches

The magazines show up in our mailboxes
addressed from databases in third world places.
They keep coming, and we keep reading,
scanning the pages for some way in
to the glossy world they invite.

Between the stories of movie stars and lovers
are pictures of wonderful watches—
gestured on beautiful wrists
in satin-colored photographs
made perfect somewhere on computer screens.
They are watches so elegant
Aztec priests would have held them up
to worship instead of the sun,
crusading knights would have stopped
their plunder to wear just one.

Looking at pages and pages of such watches,
forgotten are times when the only pictures
were left in caves, when storytellers
spoke of gods and heroes to hold the day
not knowing there was any Time
beyond the next sunrise.

And we ask what is the wonder
of such beautiful watches
without thought of Mongolian peasants,
of tribes along the Amazon,
of fishermen returning at night
on the coast of Madagascar in a world
where there are places still measuring time
by word of mouth and mothers' milk?

The Best Doughnuts in the World

Every town has the best doughnuts in the world.
The bakery that makes them doesn't need
any more than word of mouth to say so.
The sign out front has a catchy name
so when you tell the out-of-towners
that they have to try a dozen,
they will chuckle at *Buns and Bread, The Cookie Jar,*
and not the idea that some baker
in someone else's town is god of all doughnuts.

The mythology that keeps cops and commuters
coming back to balance coffee and an old-fashioned
with their low calorie meals never promises
what Swiss chocolate or a dry martini are best at.
There is no comparison between a good doughnut
and good sex or winning the lottery
that stops anyone at a bakery.

But everyone knows where
the best doughnuts in the world are;
and when a job that just pays the bills,
kids who will maybe get into junior college,
a house that has a single car garage
are in a world all their own,
nothing tastes better than the glaze
that you lick off the corner of your mouth
driving down the main street of your home town.

Sometimes All You Can Do Is Just Wonder

Tee-shirts sometimes say more than sermons.
That was the message. It didn't matter that there
was a sermon. What mattered was that the girl
giving the sermon last night at vespers was talking
with notes, but her tee-shirt was going off into
the space high up in the sanctuary the way
fireworks go off in the sky ten miles north and you
wonder what they would look like if you were
right there. You want to see the last droop of fire
into the water. We couldn't take our eyes off
Religion sucks sometimes too. Couldn't. Didn't
want to. We wondered what set off that kind of
fireworks. Everyone gets to wear their version of
politics or love or football. But religion? Was she
just trying to be funny? She must have decided
God has something to do with broken hearts or
abuse or mean e-mail. But the woman knitting
in the first pew shook her head and speeded up.
A little boy in the back wondered if you can say
suck in church, and his mother, whose tattoo
under a short sleeve showed something about love,
explained with a hug. All of which leads you to
just wonder what it would have said if Mary had
been wearing a tee-shirt on the way to Bethlehem.

God at the Grocery Store

after "Every Riven Thing" by Christian Wiman

I go to the grocery store where I find God,
I believe, on every aisle shopping
with people like me.
I'm never sure when I'll see
God there. But everywhere I look, I know why

I go to the grocery store. Where I find God
varies from day to day. Two years ago
it was at Ralphs. Today it's a Safeway. Tomorrow
I may stop at Albertsons. I know
she may be there as Allah or tell me, *I Am*. But

I go. To the grocery store where I find God
is the journey not the destination.
I nod to the woman with her baby.
A friend has a story. There is no maybe
about God being at the store. For it is you and

I. Go to the grocery store where I find God
and you will too. He cuts the meat.
She stands at the counter all day on her feet.
You meet them in produce. The girl with the tattoo
doesn't look the part; but neither do I when

I go to the grocery store where I find God.

Necessary Evil

Everyday evil meets our needs
when it comes on the screen to ask forgiveness
the way the dog, after knocking over the fishbowl,
hides around the corner and then
rubs affection on a pant leg as the guppies are saved.

When holocaust is just more history,
when genocide is too hard to fathom,
news about human trafficking in Africa
sends us to the frig to get more beer and dip.

But we are captive audience when
a deadly sin goes deep towards the end zone
with a Hail Mary hanging in the air.
We hold our breath until hands snatch, toes tap down,
wild cheers go up, and we sit back happy.

The fall of the television preacher
who took two nights in a motel room
to convert the hooker is this week's Icarus—
whose spiral down to disappearance reminds us

the bigger the better when gossip has needs,
when forgiveness must practice what it preaches
before we turn away and move on.
The Devil always knows where the camera is
and is the best guest a talk show could ever have.

Directed by John Ford

Cavalry on their Hollywood horses charged
across thin rivers after Indian extras
who had gotten their hands on repeaters.
Standing over women and children scalped and left
outside burning cabins, white dialogue
about tracking down those red savages revised genocide
into homesteading. Arizona and Texas were void
in a West that tempered hope into grit.
The sky thundered and lit up for special effect.

When the story needed a woman's touch,
young men pushed their dusty chests out
behind their Stetsons with big hands fumbling—
wanting to just talk with some young thing come west
or dance one waltz with the captain's wife.
Wardrobe made sure necklines were high
and the calico never brighter than Irish Catholic.

One-street towns and their saloons were just big enough
to hold all the cattle drives coming through,
the marshals and madams eating breakfast together,
everyone meeting the noon stage. Settlers assembled
their back-home churches for any kind of religion
they could think of to read over a grave
or make a wedding as scriptural as they could remember.

Monument Valley was no place to wander,
no place to be led, no wilderness with milk and honey
waiting in the distance—but enough space
to pretend freedom. Moses was crazy in a rocking chair
when the searchers needed to know
where to find their feathered Pharaoh to set straight.
The only commandment was about dead Indians.

And the Duke. John Wayne. The man we all wished.
The who-would-argue walk down the main street.
The gun flipping bullets. The fist and shoulder
into the belly punch. Dishing it out and then
drawling clichés to make sure it didn't happen again.
No one could have dreamed himself such a man
except John Ford, creating his promised land
where Maureen O'Hara's red hair was as black and white
as the difference between right and wrong.

The Light

At Giverny, the busses park,
and the day's travelers line up
to walk the paths in Monet's garden.
They point and remark the colors
in the morning light
but are anxious to stand in pairs
for pictures of themselves,
like models hired for the day.
From guidebooks they quote
descriptions and history
and compare what they see in the sunlight
to what was told the day before
in carefully lighted museums.

Hurried along the paths to the ponds
across the road,
they take turns politely standing
on the little bridges
and wave instructions
to those with their cameras across the water
where Monet himself might have sat
off in the trees under his big hat.

When a flag goes up on a stick
and the guide calls out directions
to the gift shop and the time
to meet back at the busses,
the ladies clutch their purses
and the men put the cameras away.
They move quickly along,
one or two glancing back
with exaggerated last looks,

never to understand
why Monet painted the ponds—
why he so often sat alone and painted the ponds.

At the Kangaroo House B&B

Before leaving next week,
I need to use the time left unwisely—
standing at the water watching gulls ride driftwood,
reading the detective novel on the shelf
just because of the red on the cover,
leaving the map behind
and driving to the end of another left turn
named *Private Road*.
I need to visit the Episcopal Church
and bring sitting alone there back home with me.

This is the first February I have spent
with time enough for timelessness
since engineering my way to a job
of highways and big bridges after college.
It's never too late, they say;
so when cherry blossoms appear too early
and winter dumps snow on them
to show what calendars are for,
a warm coffee shop a mile into town
still waits for me to stop and talk awhile
with the man sitting just where he sat yesterday.

The porch light tries to help, but fails at the steps
where darkness knows the month and day.
I am up before dawn, sitting at the window
looking out on Orcas Island, practicing island time
until the first light—knowing that
on my walk to Eastsound and back before breakfast,
the slower the better to get where I want to go.

My *Poetica*

If *ars poetica* applies, let me *be*.
Leave me alone to find the arc of beauty
along a summer coastline where the beach
is as much poetry as I dare before breakfast.
Don't ask me what I mean
when I answer a question with another question.

If you think I look like the man
sitting alone at the counter in an all night diner
and want the dark outside the window
to be the coat I wear,
even when I order ice cream at midnight,
let *finale* sit there with me.

When I read again that someone Greek
wandered until myth took hold,
I won't turn back when told
that middle age is no time to take off
into the sunset where the open road
is the American Mediterranean.

You see me often in a museum,
at a bookstore, in the concert hall
looking lost. But don't think there is danger
of my going off half-cocked
and losing my way.
I know why I am always where.

I'm looking for the answer to the Big Question
that other people say they know;
and if I look like the poem you read

in sophomore year and didn't understand,
look closer and there is *seem* waiting
beside me as I hold a pen in my hand.

Love Song in the Bathroom

You won't be able to read this poem about you and me
and not be tempted to jump ahead to the last lines.
But don't look. You wouldn't want the joy
to be at the beginning of Beethoven's Ninth would you?

Most of what this poem's about
is getting up in the morning, going to work,
getting off at five, fighting the traffic,
maybe hearing something funny on the radio
that can fill the conversation
when there's not much else to talk about at dinner.

That's the problem with the poem too—
what to talk about that isn't some attempted conceit
written just to fill the page, a few cameo lines
walking through as the man with a shadow for a face.
Most of us live lives that are just that—just lives.
The Hamlets that big books write don't go to work
every morning and watch the news at night.

You're anxious to look at the last lines now.
But first go into the bathroom. Take the poem with you.
Practice your best shower voice.
You may want to go back and read from the beginning.
You may want to sit where you usually sit
when you read in the bathroom. Either way
you're getting to what it's all about; so read on, out loud.

If you don't know what to make of all this
just suspend your disbelief. Think of this poem
as yours and that it has been published
in *The New Yorker*. Pretend it has been included

in a collection of your poems put out by Putnam Press.
Imagine yourself at a microphone
in front of an adoring audience in Stockholm.

After you finish, you may read back over it
and think to yourself that this poem isn't really fair.
You're not just another man losing his hair.
Believe that artifice is just as good as art.
If you say it's not what you would write,
think of it as a place to start.

Now stand up. Look in the mirror.
Face the face that meets you there. Think
of a deathless love song. Sing it softly, loudly
if you dare. Maybe go to the kitchen and eat a pear.

When You Need a Mountain

When you need a mountain to scale size
into a life of nine to five and paying the bills,
go to Rainier. Chose the route through Morton
on up to Packwood. Along the way,
watch off to your left what the hills
are doing on a summer day of white clouds.
In the national park on the road through the woods
before the climb, watch the trees and sunlight
in their love affair. Stop at one of the waterfalls
that give the Cascades their name and watch
how water does what you would like to do
with your life when it needs a cold shower.
When you get to the turn where everyone pulls off
to stare, get out of the car and just stand there—
and watch the mountain as it rises
into the blue where you would go if you had wings.

II

The Third Heaven

...a man...was caught up to the third heaven.
        II Corinthians 12:2

The third heaven opens
on a long stretch of road with the map put aside
after a stop for coffee. There is no up
there in the sky anymore. Any heaven on earth
ended ten years ago
looking down at the lifeless crib.
The radio voice talking about Roswell gives no clue.

It is there inside the car
on the way towards the start of day coming up
over the Oregon Cascades. It is there
lit on the dashboard to tell secrets
about internal combustion
if not about the soul.
                          It isn't about any road
to Damascus. It isn't about anything
newly written.
                  It is about the knowing
that comes just before the leaf moves
sideways rather than landing straight down
under the tree because of whatever the wind is.

It sleeps in the passenger seat
where she murmured a reminder
before folding the map. There is no
navigation now. There is a quiet more distant
than any memory of then or there;
and with my two fingers and a thumb I steer
time and place holding on for dear life.

Telling of Miscarriage

A doctor believed the sales rep, and an IUD
twisted the sperm and egg of you into something
wrong. It is so long ago I remember only the note
with the phone number, and me wondering
what autumn meant when I called.
Who writes anything down after the rush
to the hospital and the meeting in the hallway
to tell you what doesn't need saying?
Today I am walking with your brothers and sister.
You would have fit nicely into the years
between two brothers and maybe been
in the right places at the right times when
we didn't understand either of them. Maybe you
would have helped us look at the world differently
when a sister came and we finally switched to pink.
You might have helped through all the winters.

But the world moved on that day.
Fetus and placenta went somewhere unspoken,
and we never asked boy or girl. We wept.
We accepted the way lives can go—
as we had learned to do from stories about relatives
who had to move on out there on the prairie when
such things happened with no doctors around.
We tried again, not expecting any answered prayers.
The children have never known until now
they have a brother or sister incinerated,
still blowing across the universe
in ash that won't settle. Clouds and time
can't take away that we were ready.
We wanted you. I tell them of that day when
something said *no* and how it has taken years
and years for that terrible autumn to end.

I Never Turned Forty

It just happened in the middle of the night,
when I was sleeping off a decade
of presumed immortality.
I'd never worried about suddenness,
so sleep was comfortable.
But waking up
to a house full of toys on the floor
and children at breakfast already
waiting for me, what was I to do?
It wasn't exactly what
I'd heard the big 4-0 would be.
Squinting down the hall toward the kitchen
with everyone pretending pancakes,
touching the wall for balance,
I was late to what they had planned.
Pulling a chair to the table
where a place had been saved,
my smile barely followed
when the *happy* and *birthday*
finally clapped together in my head.
A pointed hat held on with a rubber band
under my chin wasn't a good start.
But a first photo of my new decade
was required—with me blowing
out a candle rigged on top of oatmeal.

Word Game with a Little Boy

To let him win,
or to play the big word
with five letters and a *Q*
on a triple word square
is too much ethics to decide—
and I make *ON*
up in the corner.
We show our left-over letters
and subtract the points.
He beats me by 8,
throws his hands up in the air,
and smiles all the victory
of a little boy
who doesn't need to learn
so much about losing just yet.
When we are putting the game away,
he looks at me
and asks if I let him win.
Inside the box
there must be a big word to answer;
but I say, *No*,
and he looks at me as if
he is adding up in his head
what just happened.

Nine Ten

A small boy, playing in his room,
became a frog and kissed a cat that turned to a dog
and chased its tail around a hundred times
in a scratching attack on a biting flea.
The boy snarled laughter,
thinking himself The King of Beasts,
and roared in his closet.
There, his shoes were old bones
left from his many feasts on sweet jungle delights.
He smacked loudly on sneakers
and purred on bedroom slippers.
But two galoshes fell and struck his mane,
and he hissed the hunter's bait as he backed out.

He soon forgot, and was a chittering monkey
swinging with two hands on a door knob
when his mother came upstairs
with his teddy bear called Sam
that she had sewn at the neck
where its insides had begun to show.
The boy frowned at *S-A-M* she had lettered
on its neck-patch bib and asked if his bear was dying.
She tried to explain, but he cried
and said she was lying. She finally had to count
from one to ten to make him stop.
That night he ended his prayers with,
I hate Sam! Nine, ten! Amen!

On television the next day,
he saw airplanes set big buildings on fire;
and in the weeks to come
he watched men on dark machines

drive in the desert and shoot at other men.
Soon, he fought against toy soldiers,
playing war with finger guns—and often shot at Sam
thrown into the corner with its insides exploded.

Snow White Wife

The ten year old's questions
head out the door for school
with a kiss and we'll talk about it
when you get home.
You too have questions
that haven't been answered.
The speeches at graduation
fifteen years ago sang future.
But the clothes you still wear
from those days are faded to otherwise.
A nine-to-five husband
is already too middle-aged
to answer. The minister tried
scripture and then just looked at you.
Oprah has ended her show.
This morning your conversation
with the mirror is the same
as last night—with you standing
alone again, holding
a lipstick and blush, hoping
mirror, mirror on the wall
will answer, *You, beautiful you.*

The Hole in the Doughnut

The hole in the last glazed doughnut
on the tray invites speculation,
and as you wait for the question,
What can I get started for you?
you try to think why a hole there.
Last year you faced a bigger question;
but it was about your heart
when, after the pause
that always means a hole in something,
the phone call simply said,
He has a cleft palate.
That kind of hole in the face you imagined
stopped all speculation
about Uncle Carlos or Grandpa Harold.
Over the next days and weeks,
you Googled and Bibled *why?*
until the answer ended up
the same as always
when the world isn't true or false.
You finally had to accept it was
a multiple choice test of faith.
And there were so many confusing answers
you had to just guess
that sometimes God makes things
with holes in them.

Stardust

Bits of planets, burst of stars have sifted down...
Gjertrud Schnackenberg in "Dusting"

There is no dust as sacred as the sawdust on the floor
of the bathroom where ants work in the ceiling.
The size of their work is silence.
The dark of the attic stores up what is there
until it is big enough to float down onto the tile
made of dust from a different eternity.

Who is to open the square above the hallway
and look up and in? We have had too much custard,
so the work continues until one night,
standing at the toilet in wait of a prostate,
dozing in and out of silence deeper than
the back side of the moon, I *hear*
the chewing at the wood, wetted under the roof
still leaking—a sound from as holy a place
as the scraping that softens rocks into the collections
of children on their walks down the beach.

Children can walk too where Time shines
through slits in the shingles; so the next day
we eeny, meeny the oldest up.
                            The clock
ticks him along as we follow his scoots
to the spot where the work has gone on.
Light years seem to pass until finally
a hand reaches down full of what
the big telescopes in Arizona will never discover.

You Always Wanted To Be the Indian

Whenever you needed to be someone in a movie
or a story too good to be true,
you always wanted to be the Indian.
At the Saturday matinee, you waited in the canyons
when John Wayne went marching
across Monument Valley. When you brought
out the hats and guns and spurs,
your big brother played Red Rider
and you were off to the side as Little Beaver.

When you needed to be somewhere other
than weeding the garden or mowing the lawn
for your allowance, your camp in the woods
was where you went not to smoke cigarettes,
but a peace pipe made out of an old briar pipe
with bamboo for the stem—
to look like one you had seen in a museum
where you remember thinking to yourself
that Indians always wanted to be Indians too.

Being born dark enough to be Something
after three months of summer, you chose Indian
every time all the way through third grade
when the teachers could still ask
about your parents' parents. In fourth grade
you figured out what they were really doing
was assigning reading groups—because
in those days ancestry made a difference
according to someone's best educational thinking.

Ever since, you have still secretly wished Indian
when you needed to. But then this year,
at Tabernacle Square, you went to the big building
across the street where you can research
your relatives. As a new parent, you had wondered
if it was true what Mormons believe—
that genealogy is the answer
to the question of what life is all about
and good family makes it easier to be who you are.

The second day there, you found out that sometime
back in the early 1800's a Cherokee had shown up
in the family. So what do you do? So much
of the world still thinks skin color is the best way
to tell who you are. Like any new dad, you hope
your newborn son grows up to be like his father;
but do you bring out your old Lone Ranger comic books,
where Tonto is Tonto, when your little boy
is old enough to want to be someone himself?

Filling the Conversation

Sleeping dogs lie
when we don't go there,
when the book is closed,
when the past is the past
if we only talk about
the weather and crops.
Family is family after all
is said and done.

When Cousin Mike went crazy
and took a sickle
to the neighbor boy
who had his daughter
behind the barn
doesn't need a date or year.
Six months after Gram
slipped quietly away,
the name of the floozy
from the city who got Grandpa
to sign over everything
is too hard to pronounce.
The potato salad
and strawberry pie
filling the conversation
at the funeral
after Uncle Frank's suicide
is more than enough said.

After the phone call at midnight,
the prayers at the cemetery,
the reading of the will,
the estate sale,

we go, dog-tired, back
to sleep on it—comfortable
that weather and crops don't lie.

Wordless Answer

When silence is the only answer to a big question,
when children ask in such a way
that even God would wait
for help from the angels to explain,
the little boy often tilts his head
with another question about the question—
and we slip quickly into wordlessness
looking out the window or across a field
as if to suggest that what he wants to know
is out there somewhere.

So when he asked, *Why are funerals sad
if people go to heaven?*
a catechism was no help at all
as we spoke clichés past the casket
open on an uncle gone to a better place we said.
We didn't talk on the ride home,
and didn't talk in the days to come.
The little man he wanted to be
carried on the silence
as the questions got smaller and smaller
through the years until we thought he had forgotten
about the face in the coffin.

But one day with an album of old photographs
on his lap, he pointed to his Uncle Bob
standing with me in front of a tractor
and asked another big question
that turned my head out the window
all the way back to the farm
that was heaven to Bobby and me as little boys.

Five Hundred Million Years in Our Kitchen

In the old house we bought with scrimp
and save in the Eighties, we look out on a street
where panel trucks park and wonder
if we should remodel too—at least the kitchen.

Last week we found a piece of dried spaghetti
on the table leg where Petey threw it thirty years ago.
Some of the maps are still where
we put them after we walked in the door
glad just to be home from that Colorado trip.

The frig is Fifties pink. The window
above the breakfast nook is cracked. The burn mark
beside the range still looks like the face of Jesus.
There's a wedding ring lost somewhere down the sink.

We talked the birds and bees on those stools.
The family gathered stories here waiting
for the turkey to cook. How would it look
if they all came home to find a TV built in
where the bread box hid the penny jar?

Do we try to keep up with the neighbors who aren't
the Joneses anymore—and dare ask bids on counter tops
of granite quarried from a place where heat and pressure
changed everything five hundred million years ago?

Car Quote

It tastes better with butter on the biscuit.
        Randy Jackson

I needed a good quote, so I used one I heard on TV.
I could have used a metaphor or told a story,
but a simple quote was the best way to tell her
what I couldn't explain—that I had ordered leather seats.
Sometimes something you don't need
is better understood that way. It's the same with love.

When you have a marriage of twenty years
and it's Valentines Day, why does she still want flowers?
She says it's like frosting on the cake. She knows today
a dozen roses costs more than our first kitchen table;
but the money saved by picking a bouquet
from the garden is somehow like her making me
go without butter because I've gained a few pounds.

We're talking a new car—that for a guy like me
is not a wife, but could be compared to what she was
as a lover. To use a metaphor or tell a story to explain
what I feel about that Beauty in the driveway,
with leather, would never explain that after twenty years
it's not about kitchens, or even the bedroom. It's about
needing something more than the stain-resistant
fabric seats that come with the standard model.

A Ship Sailing Around a Pear

Sometimes Madison Avenue thinks
photographs and poetry are the same,
and no explanation is needed
when what you see in the picture
doesn't make sense
unless you are desperate
for some kind of meaning,
meaning you will buy
whatever it is they are selling—
like hope or happiness
inside a get well card with a few lines
that try to sell rhyme as reason.

Someone from Holland America
must have thought
a picture of a cruise ship in the distance
sailing around a big pear
floating in the middle of the ocean
was enough goofy to make people forget
about Disneyland or Las Vegas
and pay their money to sit for hours
staring at big water the way the Dutch did
in their sailing ships when all of Europe
was out on the new, round world
claiming their piece of the pie.

The picture was inside the back cover
of a travel magazine in the waiting room
where I had sat alone
staring at the walls for two days.
The magazine's front cover was torn off;
so the back cover clinging there

was as remarkable to me
as my wife barely alive upstairs
where intensive care was doing all it could
to buy Manhattan and call it New Amsterdam.

Strawberry Anniversary

You are looking at the dessert tray where
a chocolate mousse is topped with whipped cream
and a strawberry riper than an eighteen year old girl.
You flash back to the home place
where the garden wasn't Eden, but the parents
made sure the berries and fruit trees
produced in Biblical proportions—and you dreamed
of the perfect girl up and down the rows.

You met her working at Yosemite
after your senior year, but you've never asked
if her parents had a garden; so you don't know
if she knows what you mean when you say,
You're prettier than a row of ripe strawberries.
You wonder if she can read your mind
when you come up with something like that
to compliment twenty-six years and four kids.

Looking at her sitting there
in her little black dress that fits the occasion
especially well just off the shoulders,
you choose the mousse—and the strawberry
is Tiffany on a chain around her neck with gold links
you hope go all the way back to the first time
the male of the species scuffled up to the female
with more than survival gnawing at his stomach.

III

Love Poem

You want to write a love poem.
You know it's next to impossible to write
a good one, so you decide to tell the truth
and let it be bad, sentimental, flowery,
too junior high to let anyone read,
full of all the words in movies
that bring out the tissue.

You start with description of her face
that hasn't launched any ships
but was the face that stopped you
in your tracks when you first saw it
getting on a bus where she was sitting
at the window in the second seat
across from the driver.

You knew when you got on
you would sit as close to her as you could
and find some way to talk to her,
to tell her that you weren't trying
to pick her up—but that
you wanted to sit close to her forever.

You write careful words about the pit
of your stomach that drops somewhere
whenever you see her naked
or touch her when you know she wants you
to touch her. But you worry the children
will know the two of you do such things.
The words get out of control and you delete.

You open the Thesaurus
to find synonyms to tame the wild sheets

that feel like summer clouds
when the two of you lie there smiling
afterwards the way God must have smiled
when Eden was still perfect.

As you get close to the finish,
you want to sum it up with something
timeless, something that gets at what
even Shakespeare probably had trouble with.
The beauty of a face, the yearning
for the physical have words that are a start.

But to describe the forever
you first saw that day on the bus
can't be done with language—unless
it goes silent the way grandpa just looks
at grandma and smiles something
that looks like a *thank you* when
they are alone and no one else can hear.

Reading over the poem,
you know you are writing too much *tell*
and not enough *show*. You know
there is cliché all over the place.
You know you have failed to say
anything new. You give up.
You don't save what is on the screen.
You just turn, and sit there looking at her face.

You Looking at Me

You are me on the walks I take.
There is no need for a mirror
or photograph. If the eyes
are the window to the soul,
that look you give me
staring as we approach each other
is the story of my life. How I know
what you are thinking is simple.
It is what I have thought all along
about your way of looking at things.
It is blank the way the horizon
opens across the water on a long cruise
with me sitting alone on the deck
after the buffet. I am on the way
to the Greek islands where no one
knows me. There I will use cards
with my name on them to buy
what the brochures tell me
of happiness. There I will sit
at café tables with you looking at me
the same as you are now
as I round the corner and keep walking
as if the sidewalk were eggshells.

At Fifty

Maybe the worst thing you have ever done
is cheat on a test or lie to your wife
about the cost of a hunting trip. Maybe you have lived
in Wisconsin so far north you can't fathom
the kinds of lives the people in *People* lead.
You have always sat up straight without being told
and claimed for taxes even the money you made
for some wood boxes you sold at a school craft fair.

Yesterday, opening day, you got your buck
just twenty miles from town,
and you are finished dressing it out this morning
in the garage, still a little drunk from too much Miller
on the way home last night. The meat is wrapped
and arranged like a finished puzzle in the freezer,
but you don't want to spend any more time
to take care of the head and legs and bones.

You've been thinking about it for awhile,
and you don't much want to spend more time
on church council or washing the car every week either.
Tomorrow is pick-up day, and you stuff what remains
of the easiest deer you've ever gotten
into the green can with the hind legs sticking out.

Truth or Dare

I listen to country music
the way I used to read girly magazines
under the covers with a flashlight.
In the car on a long trip to somewhere,
the sound of a guitar and a girl
giving heartbreak a bad name
is the kind of dangerous behavior
our Methodist parents warned us about.
But I am like the moth to the porch light
and turn it up to the level of myth.
I've never had a drunk girlfriend
or been in a bar fight that ended up in jail.
But when I listen to the broken dreams
I never dared, I am just about
the happiest man in the world.

Any Spring

The neighbor's cat touches its way
in and out of the row
of daffodils I dug down last fall,
now up and in the way
where she comes every day
to toilet herself under my window.
So polite she is, but
now confused by such color
rubbing her along
as she pushes the usual dirt back and forth.
Behind a drift of leaves composted
against a branch downed,
she hunches into the earth watching
for any passerby
who might scold her gardening.
I too touch, touch among the days of life
sprung up from the past,
nervous to be noticed,
worried that someone will see—me
digging through the magazines and books
on the shelves under my window,
hunched above the usual words
buried in the pages of my notebooks,
back and forth to the mailbox
for some response to poems
sent off in the fall, waiting for any spring.

Something Bigger than Me

If ever a poet retells my life in verse,
I want something big and brawny on the page
roaring like the Columbia before all the dams,
stretching the Palouse to an infinity of wheat.
The first lines have to be stronger than Charles Atlas
before a ninth grader told me those magazine ads
were for pansies. The rhymes at the ends of lines
need to be masculine the way *god damn*
sounds like poetry even The Man Upstairs
will understand when a thumb and a hammer
are on a roof. There can be no lemonade
poured pink over crystal similes.
I want metaphors of red meat to drip with blood.
Enough of the salon audience knitting
while they listen to laments and longings.
Let something be said about the fist fight
we men secretly want to have with life,
the horse we want to break and ride bare back.
Let the last lines strip down to naked
and wrestle with something bigger than me,
the way Greeks and Romans
wrote about real men and gods in the struggle
to find any kind of meaning in the universe.

Answer to Cancer

In his last days, he asked that poems be brought
And read aloud. He also wanted whiskey.
It was just to hear words that might apply;
And he said he was feeling rather frisky.

He was dying of another melanoma,
So we gave him his choices as he chose.
The poems brought by family and friends
Were as familiar as the one about a rose.

Thus it ended with him and us—and the poems.
He remembered one from an English class
And asked it read. With each line about
Lilacs in bloom, he turned and sighed, *Alas!*

He drank and hailed the athlete dying young.
He toasted the ball turret gunner. He railed
Against the night. He crossed the bar and died.
Together, we agreed to carry on—and wailed

A final, wild lament. We bawled in the garage.
We staggered to the back yard and bayed like hounds.
We toasted the neighbor's dogs barking with us
And collapsed—howling, giggling on the ground.

We knew he would approve our silliness,
For he answered neither fire nor ice.
We knew he would have thought it *apropos,*
For he died drunk on the milk of Paradise.

December Morning

Low hanging ducks waited the wind and then
aimed their landing down from the clouds,
through the trees, over the house, and onto the pond
silent at the back of the lot where
I carefully gardened in the dark of December.
Two touched the water with the gentleness
required of such a place at such a time,
while the third splashed feet and wings at a landing—
past and then up again out through an opening
at the end of the neighbor's yard.
It was the middle of the morning and no one else
was home to know what might be wondered there.
I stopped my gardening and waited for a metaphor
or a memory that might take me back
into the house to write of philosophy or beauty.
I knew that ducks come out of a winter sky
mulched with the clouds of another dead year
carry meaning with them—perhaps to edge the day
or trim meditation into a theology of balance
between two ducks landing and one flying on.
But nothing came. A dog wandering turned its head
but didn't bother more. A darker darkness moved
above the sky on the jet stream down from Canada.
Rain suddened across the pond for a few minutes
of hurry and wait on the porch. The ducks waited too
under the droop of a Japanese Maple never cut back,
low over the water as a place better in the rain
than a pond. Such a cloudburst and ducks landed
would surely have held my gaze inside at my desk.
But outside in the yard, where two ducks had stopped,
it was a day better for pruning than poetry.

Shadow of My Father

My father is in the garden again.
I assumed he was gone forever
after he collapsed behind the tool shed
and I finished school and moved away.

Over the years, there has been no place
for growing anything.
It was work in big buildings.
It was small city lots.
Supermarkets were always close by.

Stepping into a row of rhubarb
where I come to volunteer
in the community garden,
he kneels down the way I remember,
silently, the same as in church.

With the morning sun slanted
on my shoulder, there he is,
right beside me,
as if praying for my very soul.

Girl Walking in Wallace, Idaho

If a thing cannot be disproven, it is thereby proven.
From the mayor's 2004 declaration that
Wallace is the Center of the Universe

At the center of the universe, a girl walks
out of the corner of my eye and turns an alley
into a promenade of slow pauses and steps careful
to continue. She triggers questions I have
about a town where old mines and buildings
on the historic register hold Time in place.

In a place where proof needs nothing more
than declaration, the manhole cover on the main street
marked with east, west, north, south, and nowhere
is a town's importance. Standing here posing
for The Photo, if I follow my instinct
for loneliness, will she turn with an, *Excuse me,*

and mean me? Is her tomorrow another yesterday
when the ski lifts and bike paths are empty?
Does holding hands on Friday night go anywhere
but the back seat of a car? Is she proof that small
towns are not the center of anything—that her universe
is small enough for the mayor's joke to work? Maybe.

Or the proof may be in the pudding she will make
tonight alone in the house while her mother works
the late shift at the little store off the exit from I-90.
The sack on her arm may hold new clothes
for a trip to Hollywood she dreams—this girl
in the small town where Lana Turner is long gone.

El Segundo Dog Park

Once you've seen it, you know why
God created Eden. The world needs places
perfect in what they are, nothing else.
At this place, running for a block
next to the Imperial Highway,
overlooking LAX, created by city fathers
for mornings before the office
and evenings when neighbors
need neighbors, the dogs are
our fishes of the sea, the fowl of the air,
the cattle of our town. The time here,
back from the East of everywhere else,
with our Roccoes and Dukes and Phoebes
and Trixies and Fluffies, over there a Max,
is every morning and evening of our lives
when we still have dominion over *something*.

In the Mind's Eyes

Beauty is measured in coffee spoons too
when half-empty cups sit at a coffee shop mid-morning
after all the good jobs are at their offices
and your best friend is your dog.
He's outside where a bowl of water is there
for his half-full life with you. Neither of you
is a purebred, like all the SUV drive-throughs.

The two of you are quite a pair, down the sidewalk
every day like clockwork to sit for awhile.
Maybe someone will stop and say something, anything.
You work grave yard, sleep a couple of hours,
then walk the dog the same route at the same time
hoping routine will lead to that moment in movies
where the girl and the boy are thrown together
by the turn of a corner or tables next to each other.

Today hope isn't any more or less the same,
but the barista notices your new shirt.
The guy finished with his newspaper offers it to you.
So the woman in the corner
with her face buried in a book of lost chances
is worth an *hello* as you pass her on the way
to your usual place against the window.

She looks up and smiles the way your dog
seems to smile when you get home from work.
It's enough. There and then, it's your cup and hers
on a morning when walking the dog can wait.

She really likes your new shirt and says the color
matches your eyes. No one has mentioned your eyes
since your mother used to tell everyone
they were the prettiest eyes she'd ever seen on a boy.

Listening to Diana Krall

Satellite radio with its hundred stations
lets you choose where you want to go—
back to the 50's for rock and roll
or to Vienna for Beethoven
there on the six buttons below the dial screen.
Number 3 is smooth jazz, and you decide
Diana Krall can take you wherever
she wants. It would be the same
if you heard her in a coffee shop or sitting
in a waiting room. That kind of voice
is the west wind that tempted Magellan.
It is the one wolf in the distance
that told Sitting Bull which way to turn
when all was not lost.
Such a voice is why truckers
late at night think they can last
another fifty miles before turning off
to stop in the lonely towns
they know are never home.
It's why you know driving alone at night
is a way to get where you will end up
after the woman you love
told you to leave and never come back.

IV

A Full Empty Nest

Coffee ready, the newspaper opened,
and the perfect woman still asleep in my bed
are enough happiness for a morning
so far beyond honeymoon
and last-minute wife cards.

The never-go-to-sleep-angry rule
applied last night, and she kissed me hard
when midnight ended a day
full of news and arguing about children
still behaving like children.

The marriage is old enough to understand
when to choose between carryover
and carry on. The woman I love
knows what I need to hear
when it's really not about me.

This morning the radio
must have played a Beatles oldie to wake her.
I hear her voice at the end of the hall
and know she will round the corner
singing just loud enough to hold my glance.

I want to talk her into the kitchen, ask her
to sit beside me, and whisper apology.
But through the door, across to the stove,
Let It Be and the sound of her slippers are refrain
from then, for now, and every day to come.

The Trip of a Lifetime

The north California coast is no place to forget.
The old highway built just above the water
and then back into the trees
requires attention more than yesterday;
but at the pull-outs to let the locals pass,
staring at the map circles a town name
from the trip to San Francisco
in the 60's. The wind lifts the map
at the fold along the ocean
as the brush of an Airstream
pulls the baseball cap off the balding
that has gone on over the years.
Damn it! is more laughter than anything.
Past and present meet driving south
on the ocean side of the fault line
where tectonic plates grinding
are as silent as the end of the scream
that followed us naked into the water
off the rocks under the Golden Gate
in our summer of love. The trembles
may or may not be trucks pounding the road.
Memory competes with smartphone debate
about where to stop for the night.
We camped in the VW bus back then.
Here and now is a Buick
with shirts hanging in the back window.
On The Avenue of the Giants,
a picnic table long forgotten in a clearing
is a place to pause. Who would think
eating our fruit and sandwiches
here would bring tears?
Under pitch and moss, initials and a peace sign

are barely clear enough to still be ours.
Through the big trees, the sun spreads
a blanket like the one we laid there.
There is no high in the cookies
we have brought this time.
There was no *then* in those days. There is no *now*
as we try again for the trip of a lifetime.

the last thirty years of Saturday mornings

with the parking more and more a problem
new waitresses less friendly every six months
who is the cook this week

the four of you sitting there
with your stories more or less the same each time
menus not needed since Reagan
always the one next to the window first

then around the table with laughter
and words about eggs one way or another
which kind of bread for the toast
maybe juice this morning

a man and a woman at the next table
wondering what all the silence is about when
two egg whites stops everything
and sheepishness creeps in

picking through cheese and potatoes
leaving some of each on the plate this time
the way Stan Musial said to stay in shape

the word *bypass* quietly as the big news of the week

Dinner Conversation

The question of who you would like to have dinner with
comes in behind the coffee and dessert, and I think Elvis.
Then I know I should be serious, and I chose one
of the men who is said to be entombed in the footings
of the Brooklyn Bridge. I always choose someone dead.

I tell everyone at the table how I identify with people
such as a Chinese worker not allowed in the picture
at Promontory Point or any of the women who sewed
all those gowns for Jackie. I have always wondered
what a woman on the Trail of Tears would have to say.

Yes, the big names would be interesting. Yes,
they would shed light on what history writes.
But I am interested in the back stories, as they are called,
in which minor characters play minor roles, die,
and then are never heard from again except when,

as a kind of parlor game, someone like me has the chance
to imagine what it was like to be nobody special—
like the six of us having coffee and dessert
on a Saturday night in a suburb of a large city
on the west coast of the United States at eight o'clock p.m.

Cliché Memories

Instead of writing a lot more that says nothing,
I'll end with a few clichés.
    Written in a high school yearbook

Four years became a lot of will truly miss you's
and good luck's in whatever you do
in the future if you follow your heart.
A not-very-good friend will always
stay in touch because he really enjoyed
knowing you. Someone you don't remember
will always remember you. The one
who signed over her face maybe because
you didn't like her anymore after eighth grade
uses the default to good luck and her name.
A sophomore didn't know you too well but
looks up to you. You have to flip back
to the junior class to figure out why someone
on the inside back cover took half the page
to thank you for all you've meant to him.
The one who remembers you as the worst
chemistry student ever doesn't mean it
and knows you'll do well in college.
The valedictorian uses big words
that are still clichés. You've been a true friend
to the mouse who always wore a cardigan
with the her bad hairdo and those thick glasses.
It was a real blast at the sign making parties
with the girl who admits with a giggle
in parentheses she had a crush on you.
The one who took the time to compliment you
on all your accomplishments stopped there.
Someone whose signature you still can't read

spent most of a page on himself.
All the made it through's and finally made it's
now seem more sad than happy.
You wish your best friend from grade school
had said something more than the lot of fun
you had as kids. The one who predicted
your name in lights someday was really,
really wrong. The girl who used a line
from a love poem to tell you what she felt then
has been saying the same thing to you
ever since she married you. You have hoped
for twenty-five years that your best friend's full page
ending with this is not good-bye will someday
be an hello and how have you been
at a class reunion when yearbook clichés
don't need to be any more true than memories.

Feathers at My Door

Anyone might have wondered the same as I
what was at my door last night.
The clichés of wind and wanderer
don't leave feathers, so it might have been
a robin or sparrow out too late.
Something had been up to something.

It was nearly midnight when I had heard
a bump and then a kind of scuffling
as if someone trying to get up
after an eighty year old fall
on the way to the bathroom in the dark.
Such sounds keep me awake too often now.

What I found when I opened the door
to get the morning paper was the same as always—
the pink of sunrise, a woman walking her dog,
a garbage truck across the street. But the cat
looked up at me as if she wanted me to believe
that feathers at my door don't mean a thing.

Ars Poetica

A feather from a nest
outside the window
floats down to the sill.
Until now,
there was only the chirping
of small birds
new to the world.
What to do with
the feather is the question—
let it blow
off into the yard
to mix with dirt and leaves
or pick it up,
finger and thumb,
and add it
to the rest of the things
I've been trying
to put into words.

The Bird Behind Jesus

The trees long gone are still deep in the DNA
of birds come nesting back every spring
high up on the ledges of tall buildings.
Downtown gardeners rig netting and shiny foil
to turn them away, for we want
no white droppings down our walls,
no pretending trees outside our windows.

But a pigeon goes on with her ancient architecture
behind the Jesus in front of First Presbyterian,
the Jesus stretching out its arms
wide with a cross in mind.
Out and back to places still draining
rivers from the glaciers left, distant places
where rainbows might touch down,

she builds with twigs and moss,
busy keeping the covenant of instinct—
finally to sit for days, just her head showing,
flickering in the eye of the news camera
aimed when a city crew with long hydraulic arms
is there to reach up and take back the flood.

No Mention

Sometimes just seeing something is enough—
to catch it in light that has shined there
the same since redwoods were small,
to watch it move in its own place
without any physics to explain why or how,
to look away and then back again
to make sure it is as real
as the meaning it would have
if art or religion applied.

Telling too much ends in cliché—
when a leaf falls in a slow dance
down to water running out
of the woods and then circling
through rocks and tangles
to a corner and off somewhere,
or when the baby tries
grandpa's walk but does better
on the dog's four legs
as it sniffs for cake on the floor
at a birthday party.

There is no mention needed
when returning from a walk
to give any more meaning
to the common things along the way
than to answer questions about the weather
and the neighbor's fence still down—
and maybe a new calf
funny underneath its mother
sucking life into itself.

My Brother

I cannot explain how the man sitting
on an upside-down five gallon bucket
at the bottom of the freeway off-ramp
is my brother. He is there every day
as I head for work on the same route
I have taken for twenty-five years.
His sign about needing food
hasn't changed for months
and is sagging its cardboard as if
it knows how he looks to the world.
Every once in awhile I give him the change
that my wife leaves in the ashtray.
When he reaches out to take it,
I know he is my brother; but
as I said, I cannot explain it—
the same way I cannot explain how I know
the woman who for twenty-five years
has left money in the ashtray is my wife.

Subdividing the Home Place

Along the ditches and back into the trees
where childhood ran back and forth,
walking quiets the moment. The rock pile
that marked the farthest out we dared go
is still there to settle any debate about
permanence—and sets a place to start.

The pond, where naked swims in the sunlight
taught so much about trust,
is gone back to fallen trees and grasses
grown up—shrunk to a small pool
ringed with so much of what happens
when absence is the only marker
of the distance from the boys we were.

The shed where we lit rolled newspaper
and pretended cigarettes between Bogart
fingers and a thumb has disappeared
into blackberries. Is the metal box still buried
in the corner where we hid promises
written for the time we would return,
to those afternoons away from mothers
who knew we weren't helping any uncles?

They are now the places of no return;
and walking, playing no cowboys and Indians,
pretending no Huck Finn,
is just steps—one in front, another,
pacing off into the thickest of the trees,
then through to the old pasture
where we dreamed the Yankees,
where voices now point here and there at stakes
and string strung across new-mown dirt.

Field Walking

Every fall I walk the fields at the edge of town
across the wild grass and low, wet spots.
It is my sixtieth birthday, and I walk again
to watch the waiting sky clouding over
for an evening rainstorm. The ground
is in its first decay at the end of the year,
and the world gives way under my step.

I am not walking the fields to get anywhere.
I am not walking the fields as some old farmer
to make certain all is ready for winter.
I am out behind the rows of new houses
before they are finished and fenced in,
just come from my take-home dinner,
to walk before it gets dark again.

I am walking because I do not want another nap.
I do not want to stare again at the news.
I am walking because it is the best place
to be at the end of another day in a week.
It is to keep from getting in the way,
out here in the fields, beyond the cul-de-sacs,
to walk where there is still long grass and deep dirt

Reading about Hemingway

Reading about Hemingway, you start
to wonder. You wonder if he believed
in anything other than being whatever
he thought made a man. After all,
he killed himself—which is the kind of thing
a little boy might think to do when he says
he'll just kill himself if you don't let him...
Well, you fill in the part about whatever it is
that makes little boys say such things.
And Papa killed himself in Ketchum.
Idaho. No one in Idaho goes by
an affectation like *Papa* rather than a real name
unless he is a grandpa. One might conclude
he killed himself because he couldn't
stand being old enough to be a grandpa.
Maybe it was his real name, Ernest.
That's a name you might find
in an English play, and if there is anything
he wasn't, it was a weak chin
and long-winded sentences. So maybe
he killed himself for fear someone
would call him Ernie, like the kid
everyone knew in third grade who grew up
to be the worst member of a bowling team.
Hemingway always seemed to be
playing a role rather than living a life.
Bull rings in Spain. Marlins off the Keys.
Cafes in Paris. And then a shotgun
in Ketchum. It makes you wonder if
he had had a name like Bob or Bill or Frank,
maybe he wouldn't have had to name

himself Nick in so many of his stories—
and then kill himself without being man
enough to leave a note explaining why.

Twenty Lines about Tools

Your backyard is the story you want told
at your retirement. You want something written

about it on your gravestone. You are tempted
to add something about it in your will.

Without something put into words
for the children to remember about all the work

you put into the rock wall, the pond
with the fountain in the shape of a Greek myth,

the playhouse with stained glass in the windows,
you worry they will forget what example means.

You hope that when the four of them
start laying out all your tools at the estate sale

as they clean out the garden shed
to get the place ready to put on the market,

the oldest boy will decide that maybe
they still have some life left in them

and put the tools back in the chest you made
out of clear oak with your own hands, carry them

to the car as carefully as good stories are told,
and find a use for them in his own backyard.

We Suburban Boys

We suburban boys never had our journey
to find manhood except on our bikes midweek
in July when the moms said to just be back for supper.
They knew in those days
the woods that was our wilderness was close enough
for us to hear the long call of our names
echoed out from the back porches
to the camps we made.

No vision quest or walkabout was part
of our bringing up. No tribe prepared us
with a dance to send us off. The only thing ready
was our bikes on their kick stands and whole days
stretching down the road the way we had heard
wilderness wandered on forever
in the stories we read about Indian and aborigine boys
disappearing into men. Our coming back from trying
was coming back to supper.

The Huck Finn and Holden Caulfield stories
we substituted for journeys never taken
were put away after high school,
and we set out with a drivers license
to prove that we had been somewhere
far enough down the road to fit us in with the men
who needed us for the mills and offices
where manhood was broken down to *Yes sir, No sir.*

But the road is always there in the windshield
every morning. The national parks are our wilderness.
River rafting with the boys from the slow pitch team
is our escape. After listening to Springsteen

all these years, we know what we missed
and often get in the car and drive off down the road
looking for the vanishing point
where opening it up to eighty isn't ever fast enough
to take us where we always wanted to go.

About the Author

Tim Sherry was a student and athlete. He is a husband and father and has been a public high school teacher and coach. He has been a high school principal, volunteered over the years in church and community activities, and is a grandfather. Always there was poetry kept private because athletes and coaches and principals and Scandinavian Lutherans don't usually do that sort of thing.

In the last ten years, with the support and encouragement of so many writers in the Northwest, he has had poems published in *Crab Creek Review*, *The Raven Chronicles*, *Seminary Ridge Review*, *Windfall: A Journal of Poetry of Place*, *Floating Bridge Review*, and others. He has been a Pushcart nominee, and in 2010 was an Artsmith Artist Resident on Orcas Island. Most recently, his poem "Of Fires" was a finalist for the Rash Award in Poetry and published in *The Broad River Review*. This is his first full-length collection.

He earned a B.A. in English from Pacific Lutheran University and an M.A. in English from The University of Chicago. He has lived in Chicago and for a short time in Europe, but has lived most of his life in Tacoma, Washington where long walks, quiet days, many friends, a close family, many travels, his faith, and his wife, Marcia, are the inspiration for his writing about the common things along the way.